My Last Day With You

My Last Day With You

A Mother's Memoir

Renee Capps

Writers Club Press

San Jose New York Lincoln Shanghai

My Last Day With You
A Mother's Memoir

Writers Club Press
an imprint of iUniverse.com, Inc.

For information address:
iUniverse.com, Inc.
5220 S 16th, Ste. 200
Lincoln, NE 68512
www.iuniverse.com

ISBN: 0-595-12385-6

Printed in the United States of America

THE BEAR, THE BOO, & THE BUG
To my babies and the ONE who made them

*~ For mother's with wee ones
who won't be wee for long ~*

Preface

"How old do I have to be to be a flower girl? Will my wish still come true if I eat the wedding wish candy instead of putting it under my pillow (chomp, chomp)?...And on and on came the questions from my four year old daughter on the way home from her first wedding.

My response, disqualifying me for any chance at Mother of the Year, was wishing she'd just fall asleep.

That was before the memory came. The memory of a five year old girl in a yellow satin dress, dropping rose petals in the isle of an old Cathedral. My first wedding.

How could the years have slipped away so quickly? How did I change from that little girl then, into the woman I am now, so unaware of the little changes from day to day? And I realized that my daughter too, would never again be the same little girl that she was right then.

With new appreciation for the little person sitting behind me, I kindly answered all of her questions, then came home and wrote, "My Last Day With You."

I

My Last Day
With You

Sometimes I wonder
Just what I would do
If I found out today
Was my last day with you.

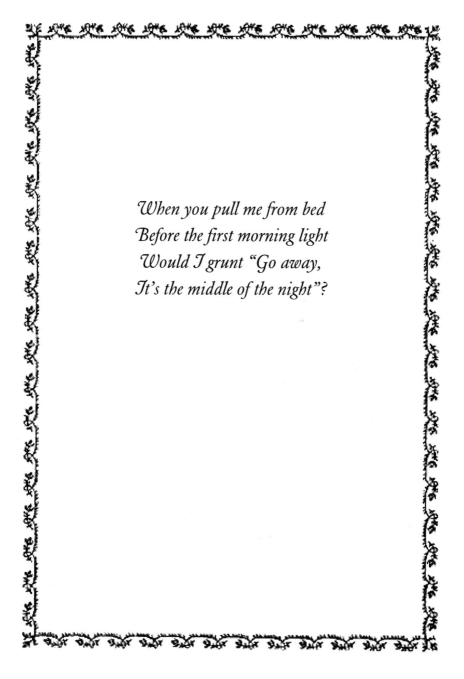

When you pull me from bed
Before the first morning light
Would I grunt "Go away,
It's the middle of the night"?

*Or would I toss back the covers
And when my feet hit the floor
Say, "Hey a new day
Let's go explore!"*

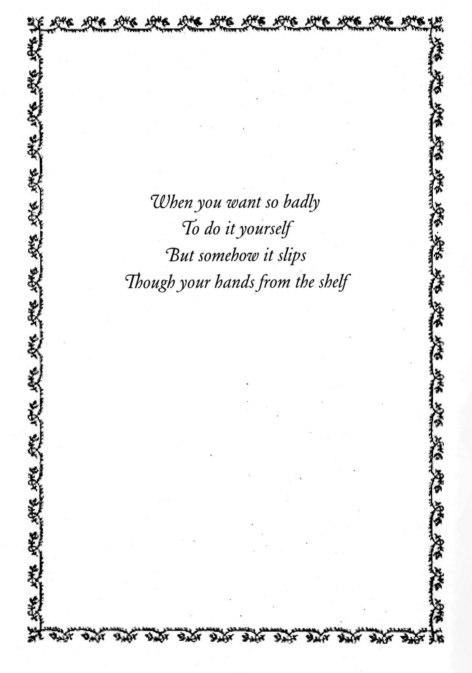

When you want so badly
To do it yourself
But somehow it slips
Though your hands from the shelf

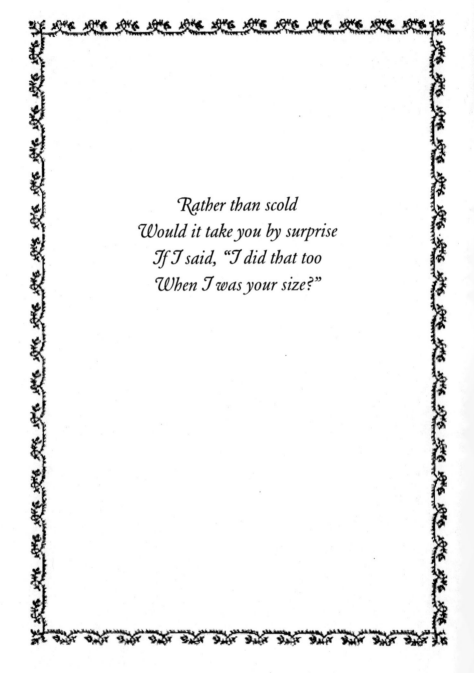

Rather than scold
Would it take you by surprise
If I said, "I did that too
When I was your size?"

When laundry and dishes
Are piling sky high
Would I see you as a nuisance
To be pushed aside

Or would I find a kind way
To tell you the truth:
"There are some things each day
That we don't like to do
But I'd much rather be
Out swinging with you."

*I wonder at night
When I tuck you in bed
With the weight of the day
Pressing in on my head*

If you were to plead
"Just one story more?"
Would I say, "No, that's it",
And pull tight your door?"

Would I sigh with relief
That your day was now through
If this really were
My last day with you?

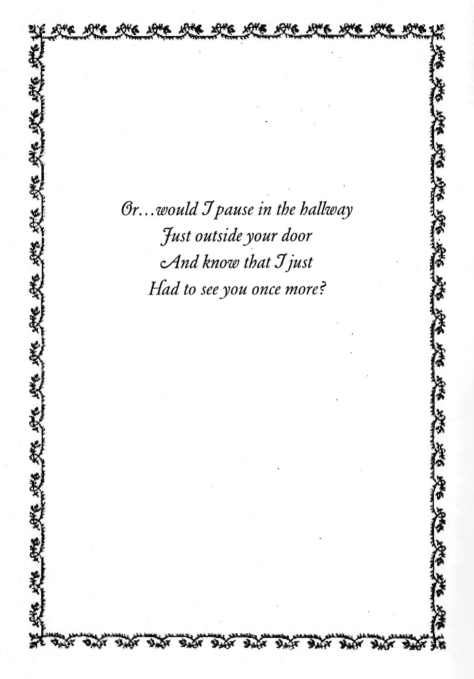

Or...would I pause in the hallway
Just outside your door
And know that I just
Had to see you once more?

And as you lay sleeping
I would sit by your side
And take your small hand
Gently in mine

With tears I would pray
You knew how much I cared
And thank the dear Lord
For the time that we'd shared....

I wish I could say
This was all just pretend
But I really must tell you
The truth in the end....

My child, it breaks my heart
But it's true
Today really was
My last day with you

My last day to know you
Just as you were
So joyful
Precocious
So childlike...
So pure

For tomorrow you won't be
The same as today
In each passing moment
We change in some way

And 'tho day to day
The changes seem few
Just look at me now
I was once small as you

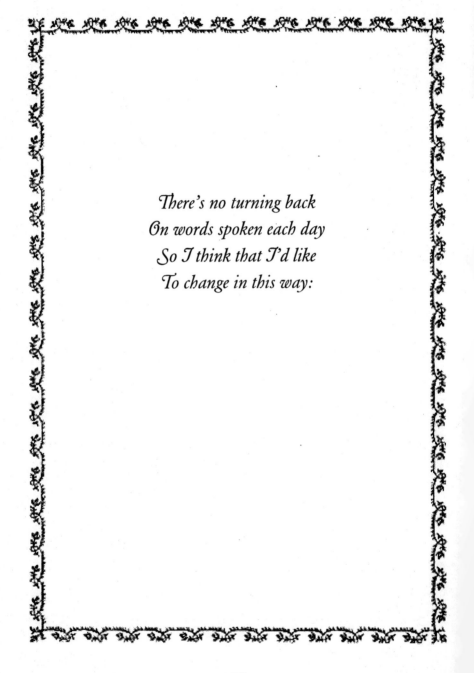

There's no turning back
On words spoken each day
So I think that I'd like
To change in this way:

I pray that we might
Start life anew
And today I will cherish
My last day with you

II

A Mother's Memoir

~All the memories written here
Are of the babes I once held near
'tho words may fade and pages fray
Within this heart they'll e'er stay ~

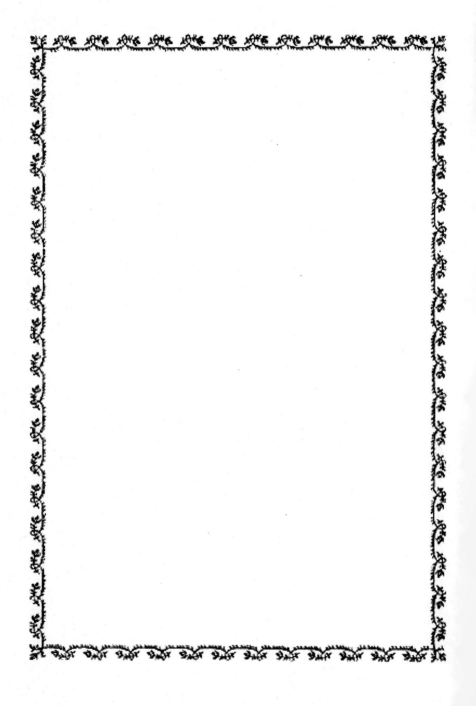

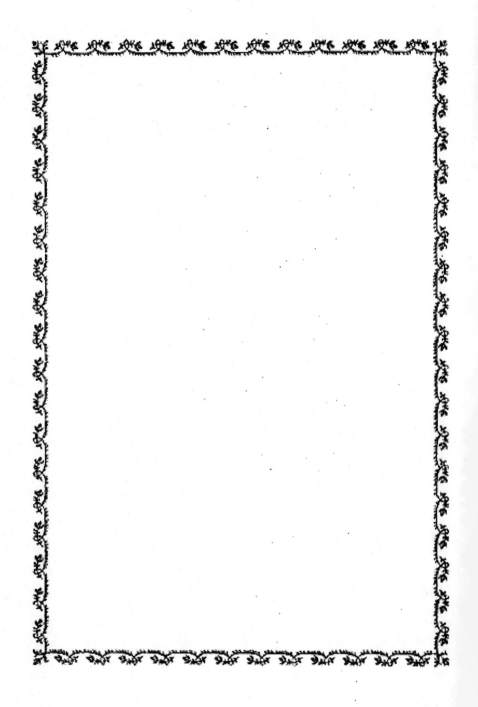

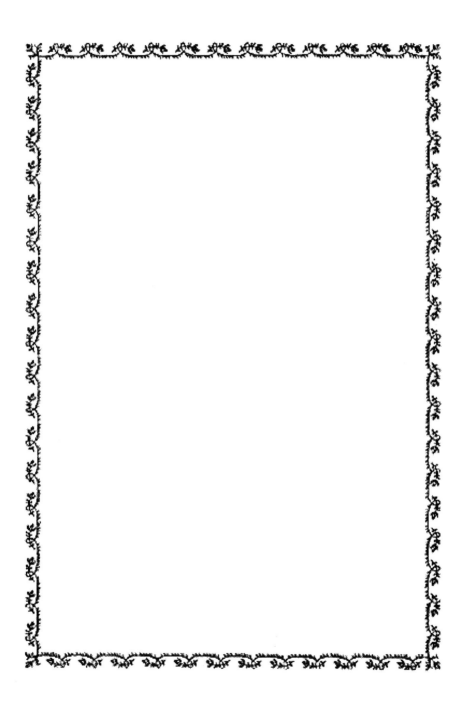

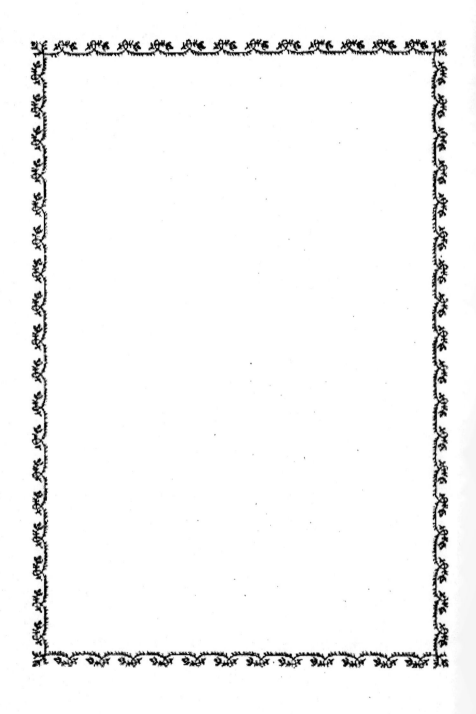

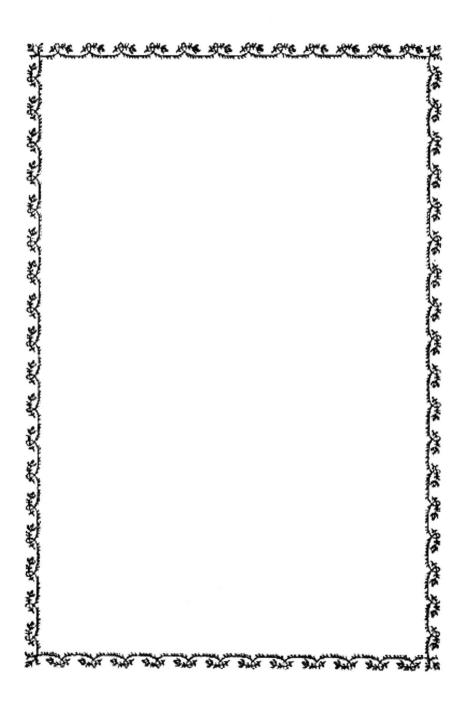

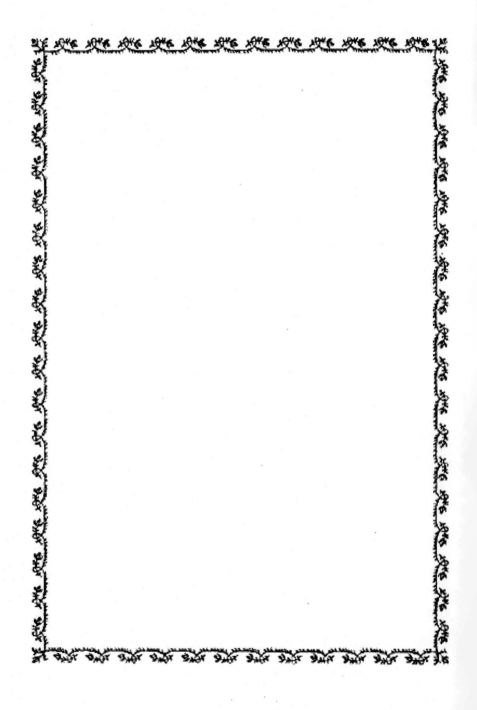

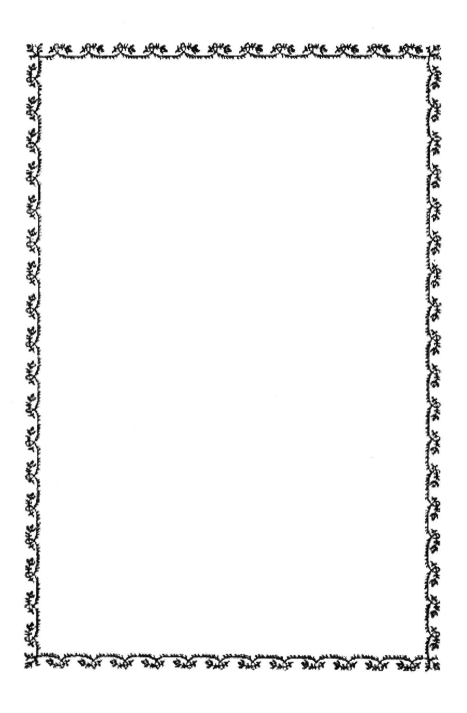

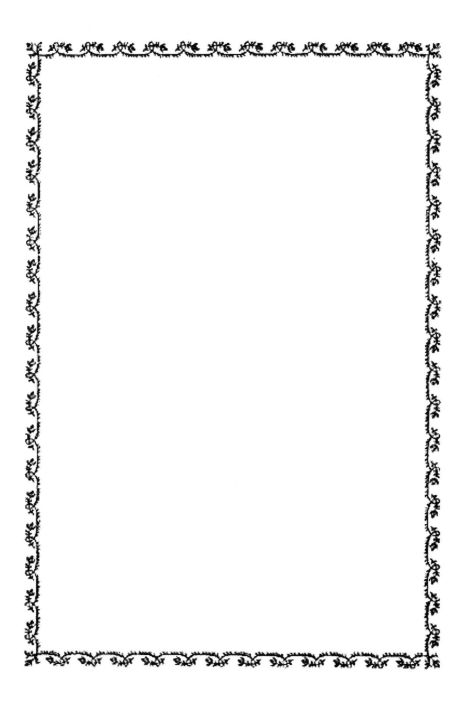

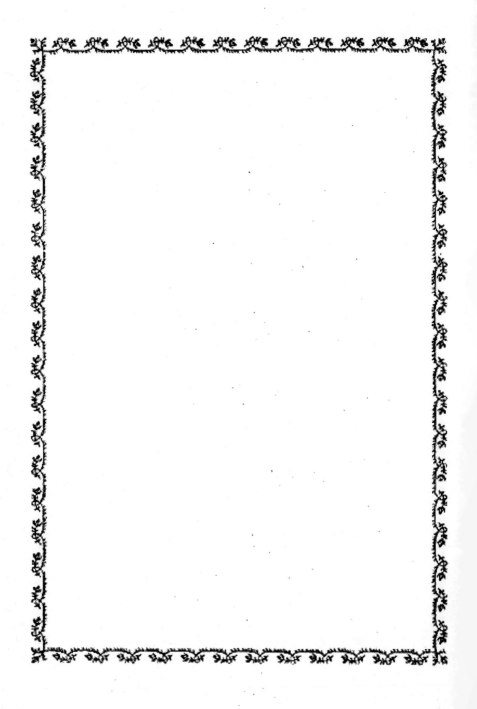

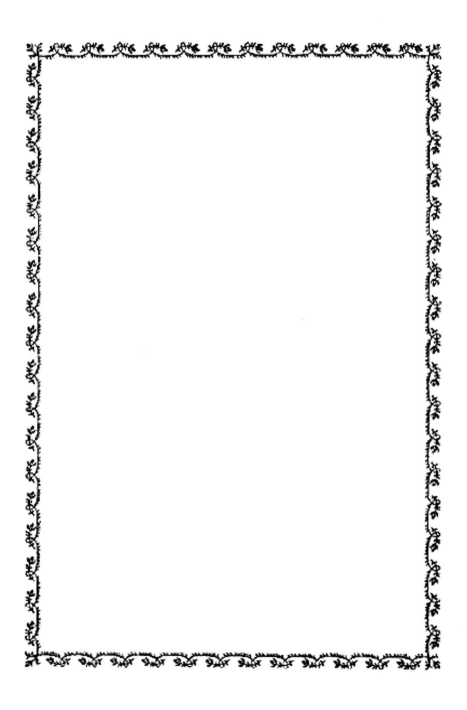

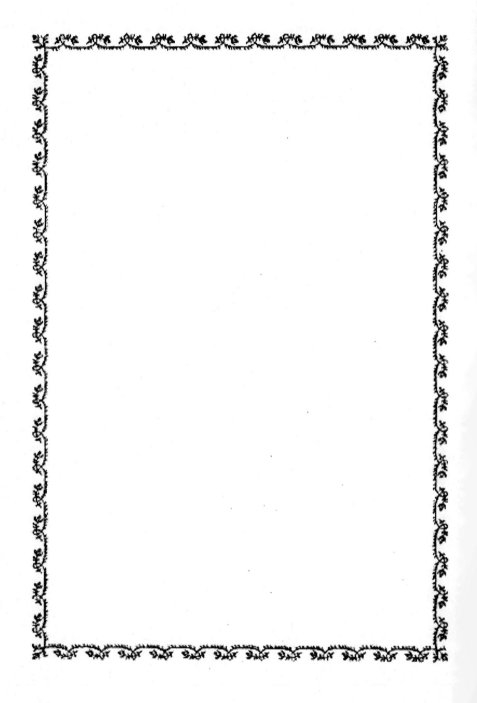

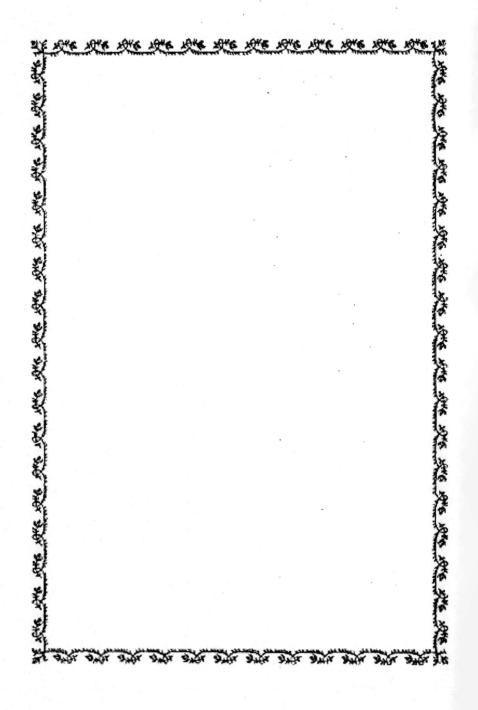

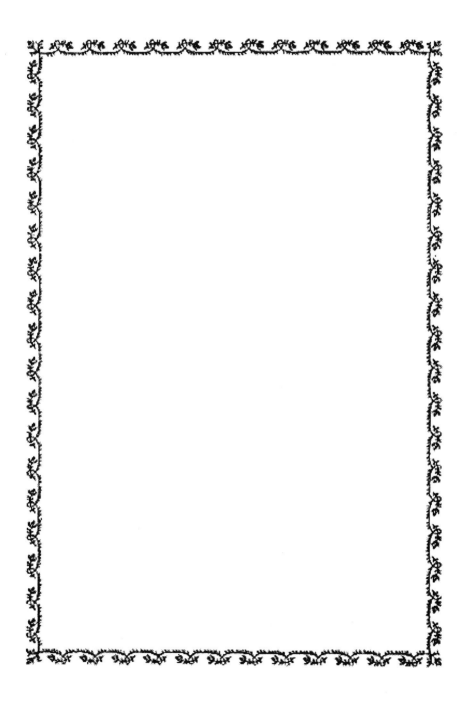

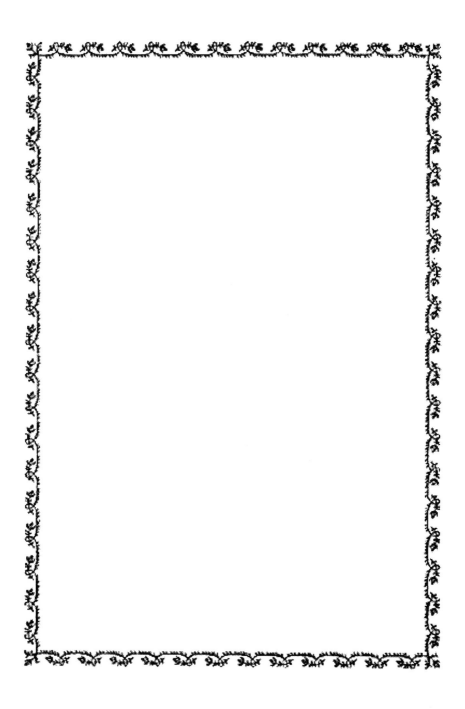

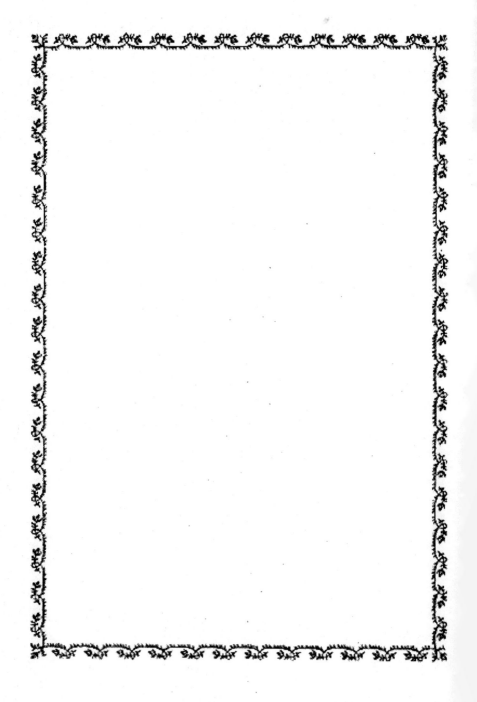

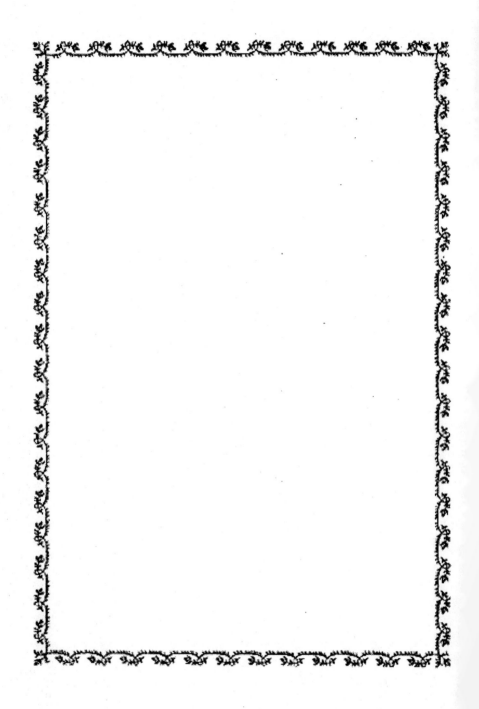

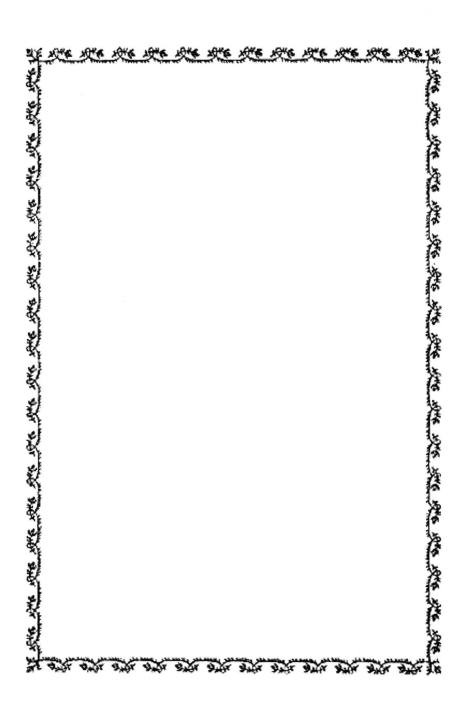

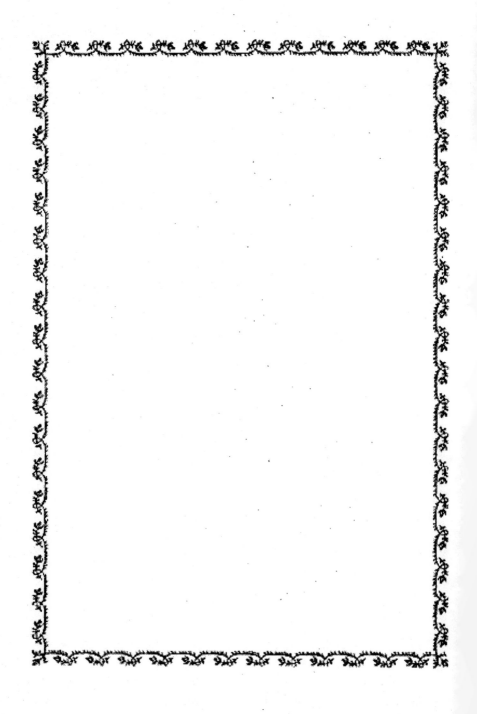

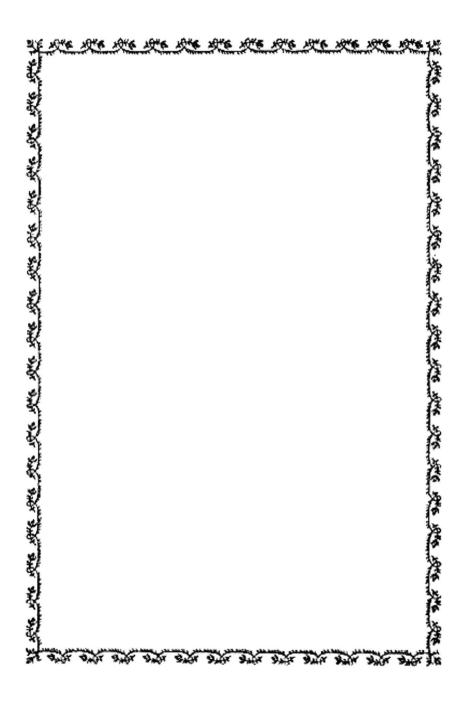

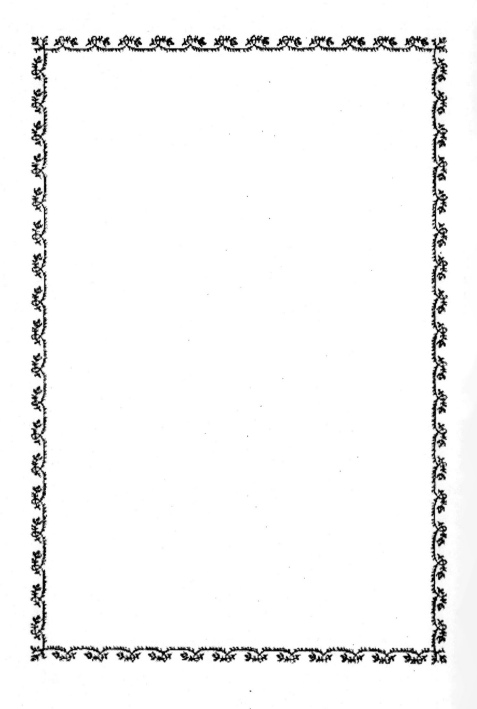

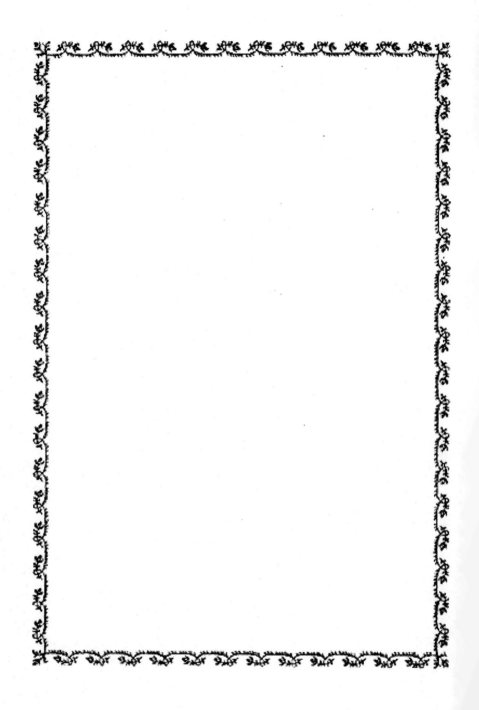

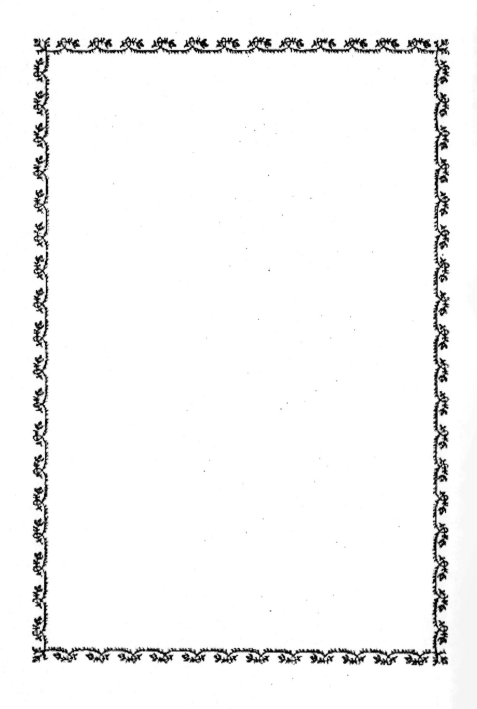

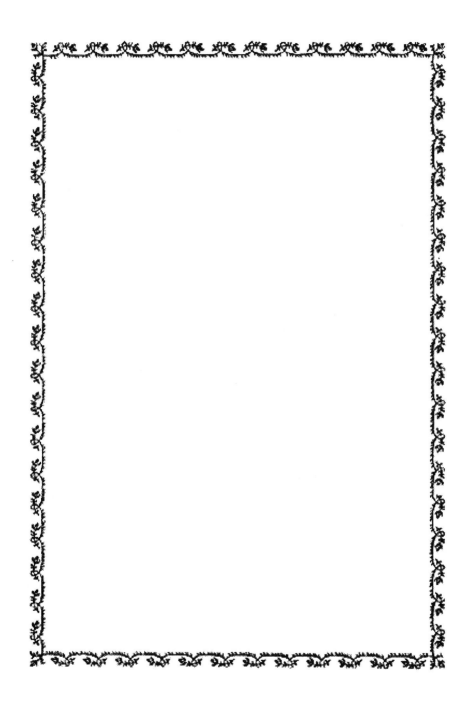

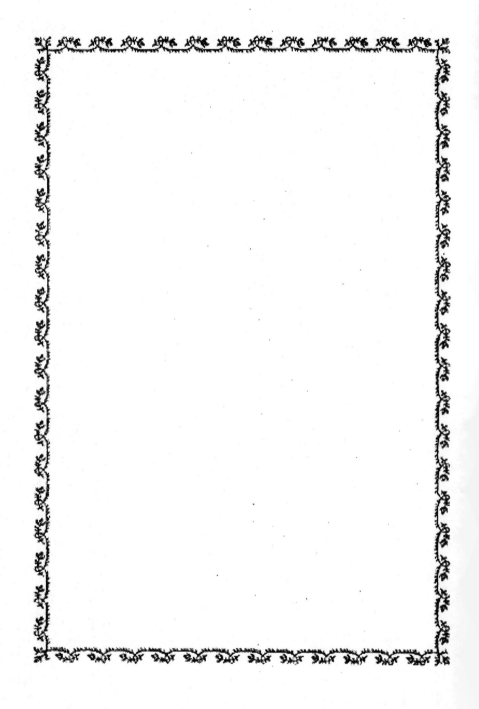

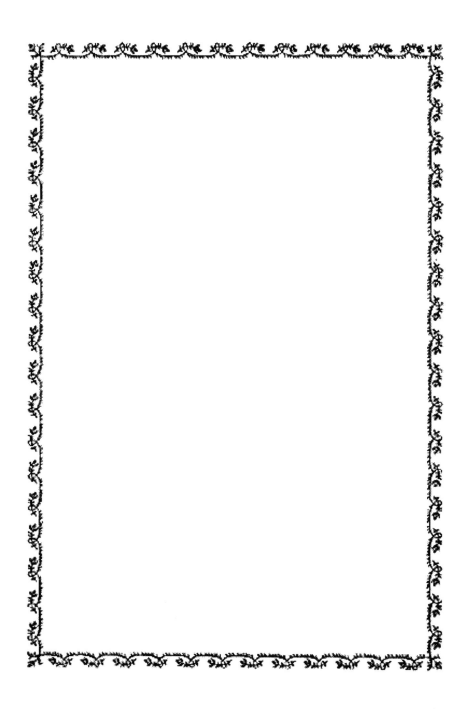

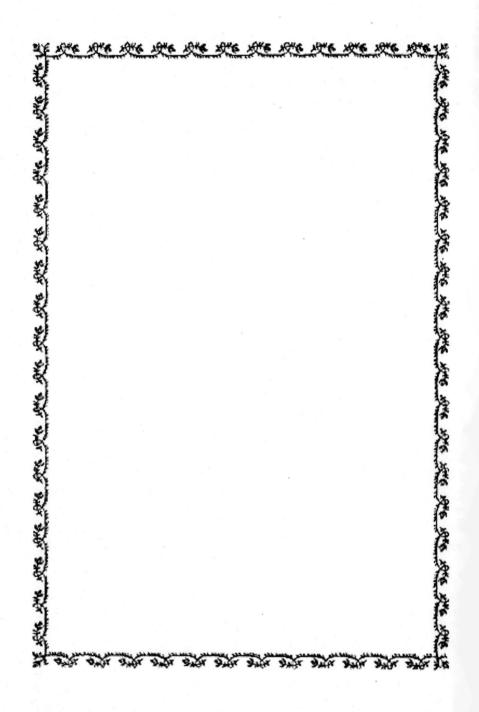

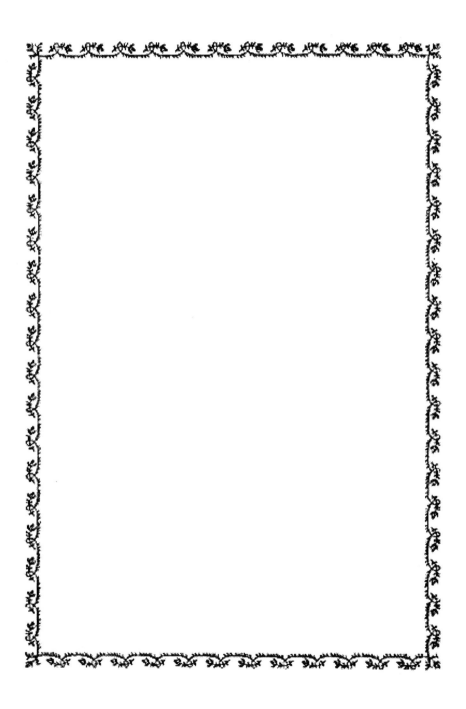

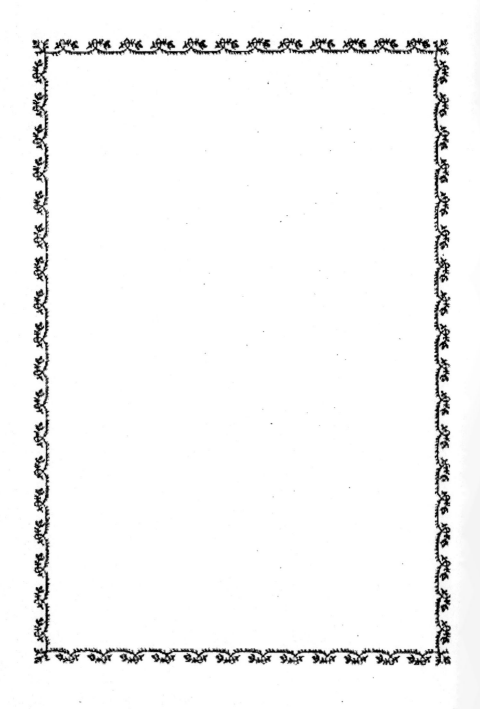

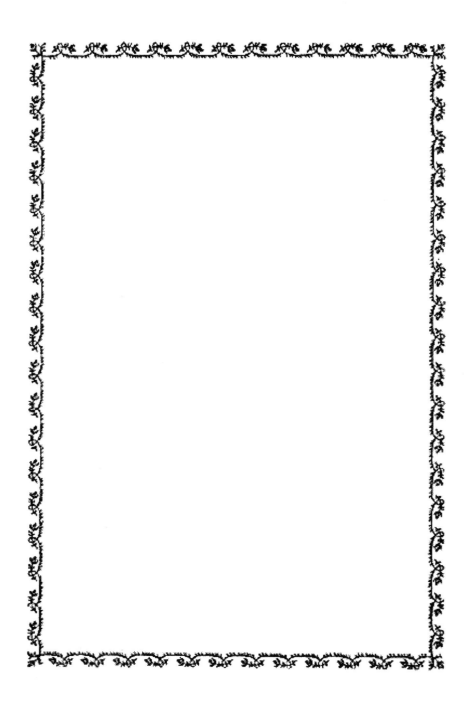

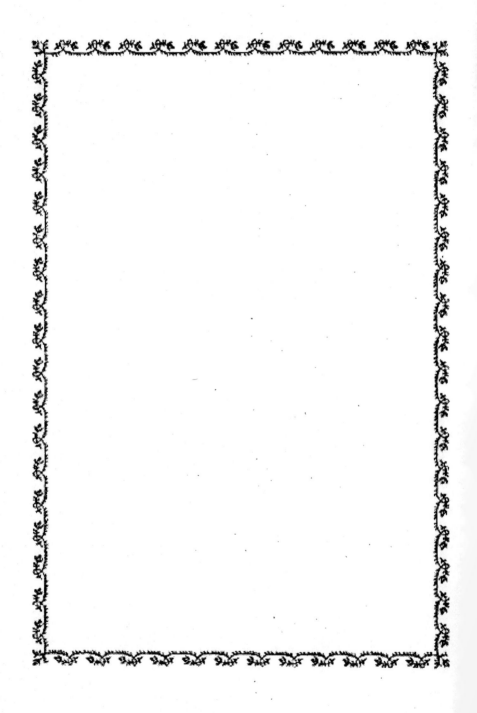

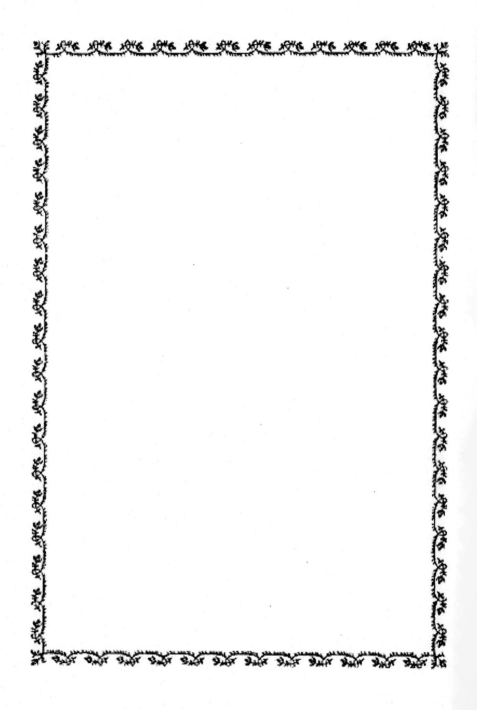

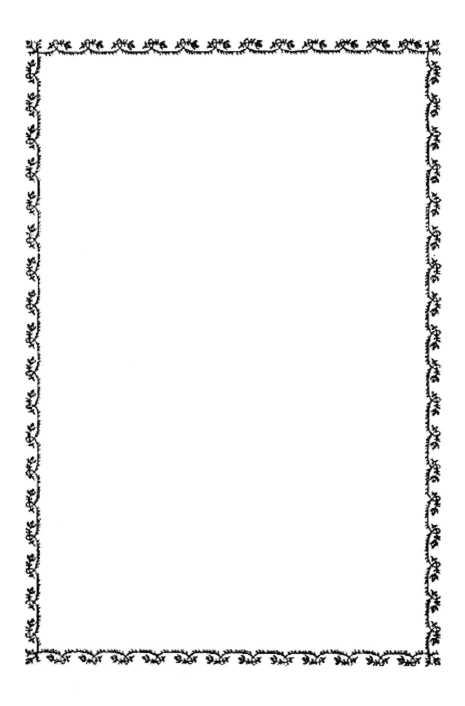

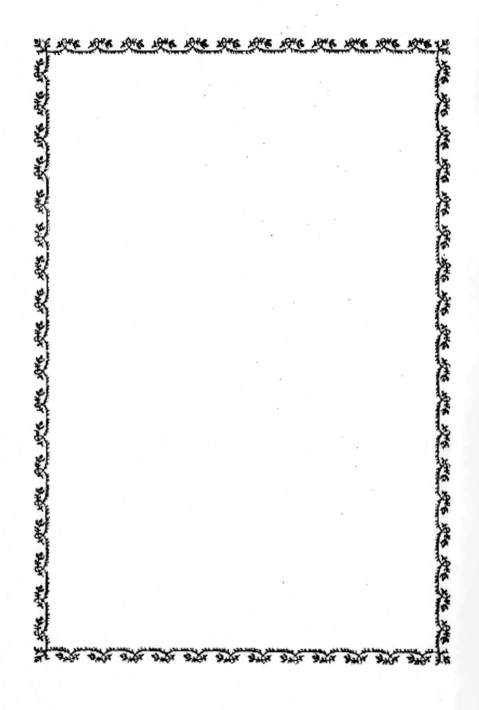

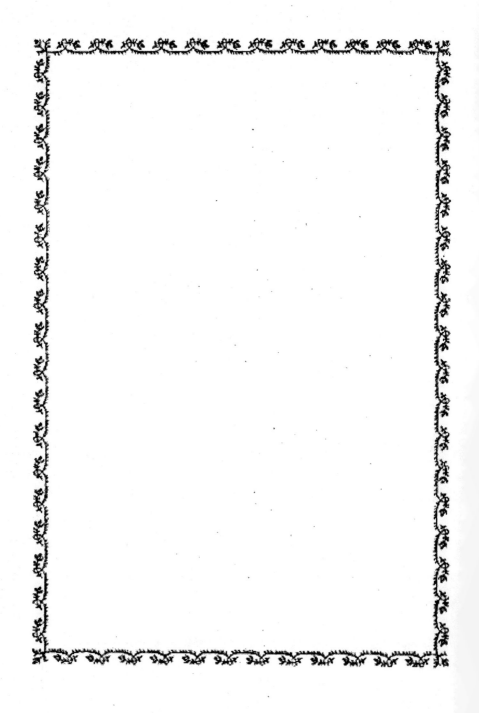

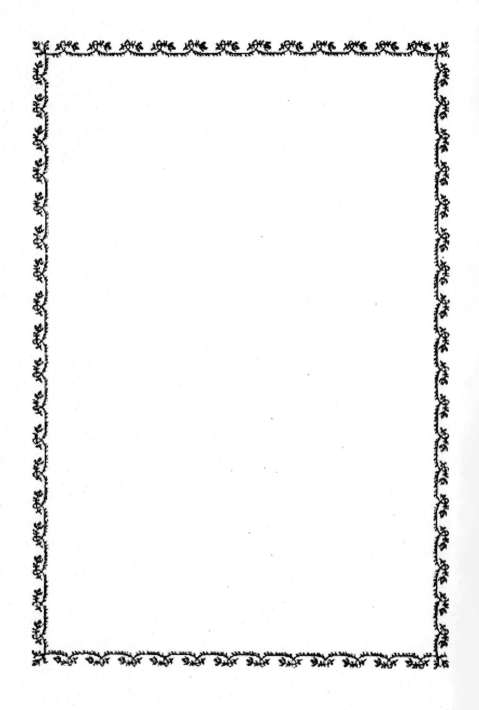

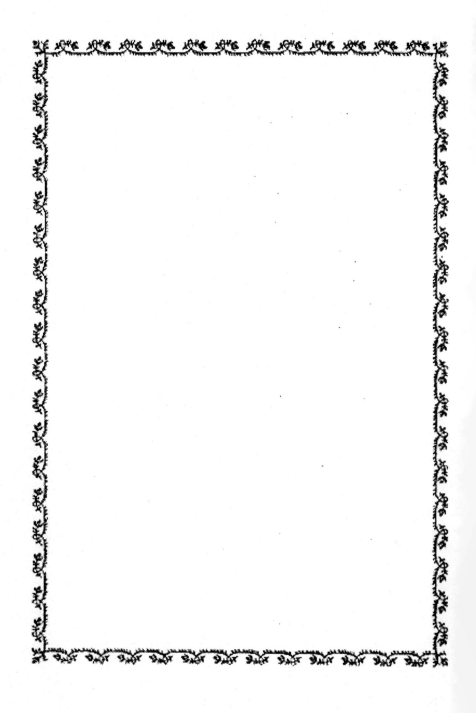

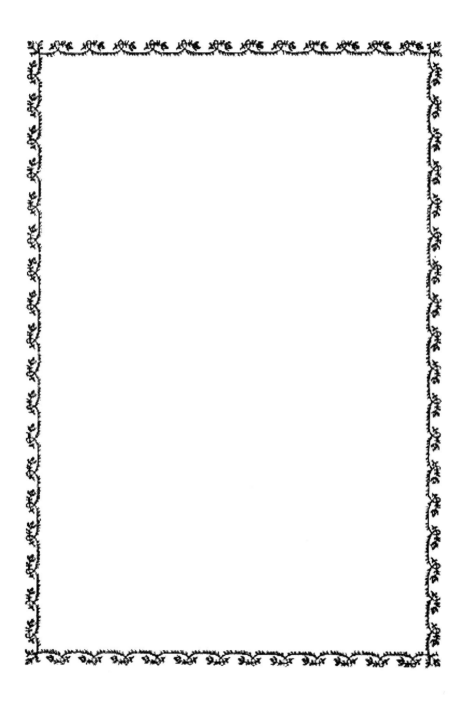

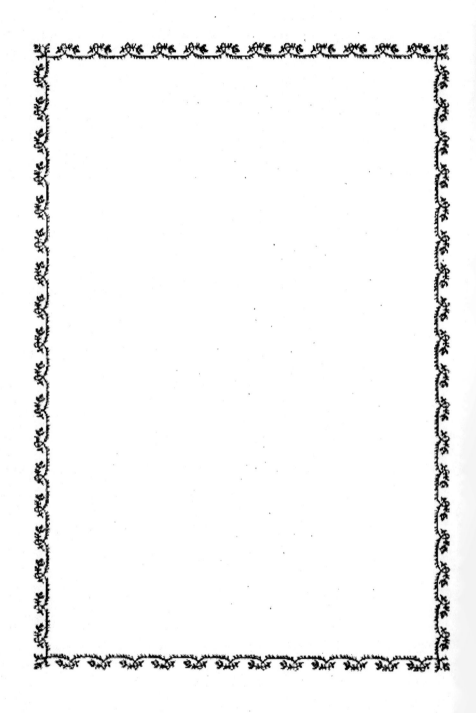

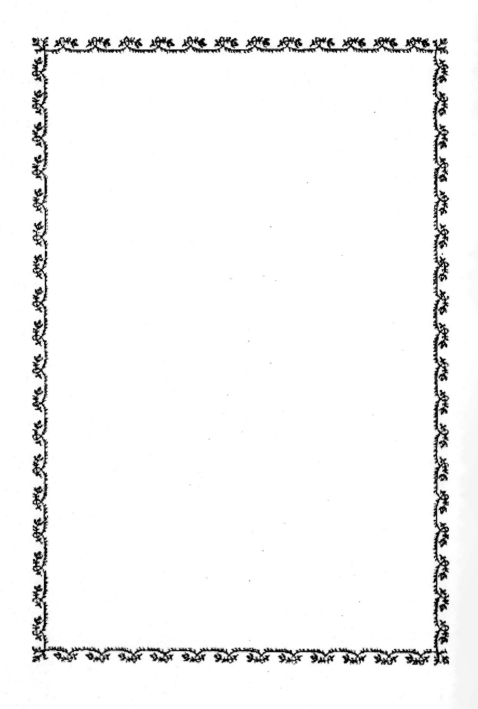

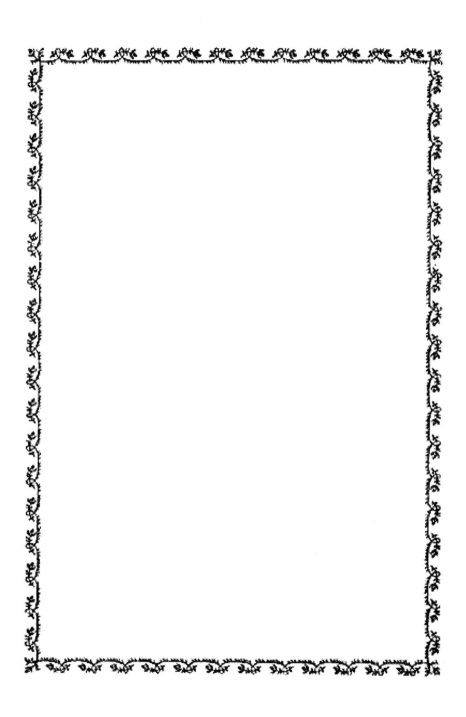

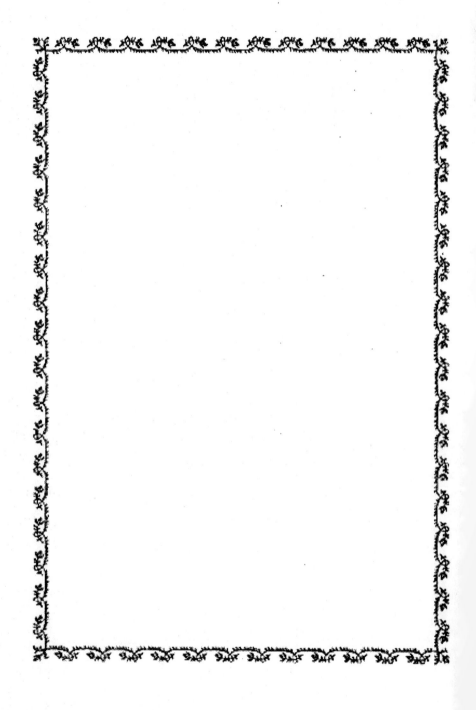

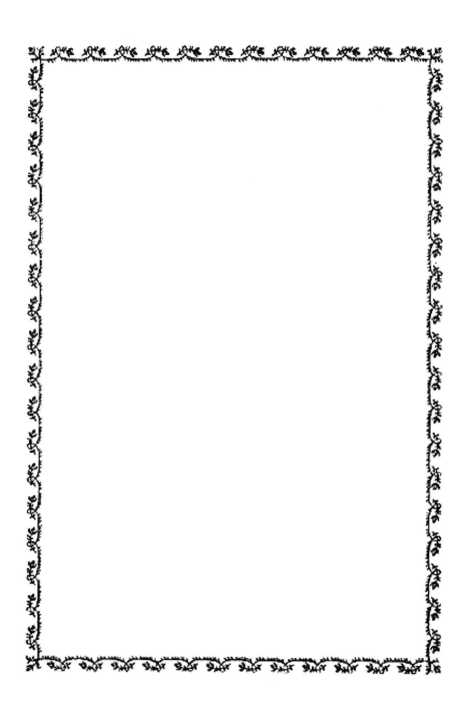

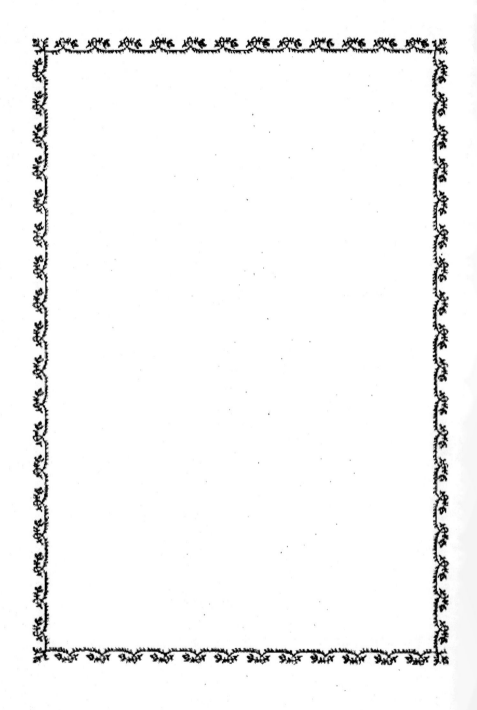

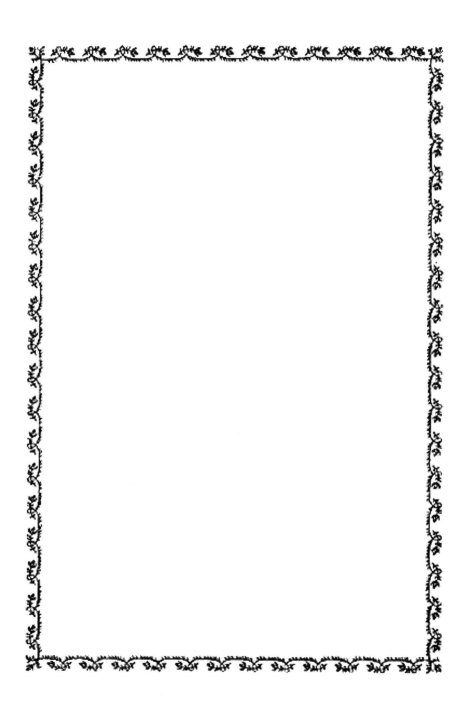

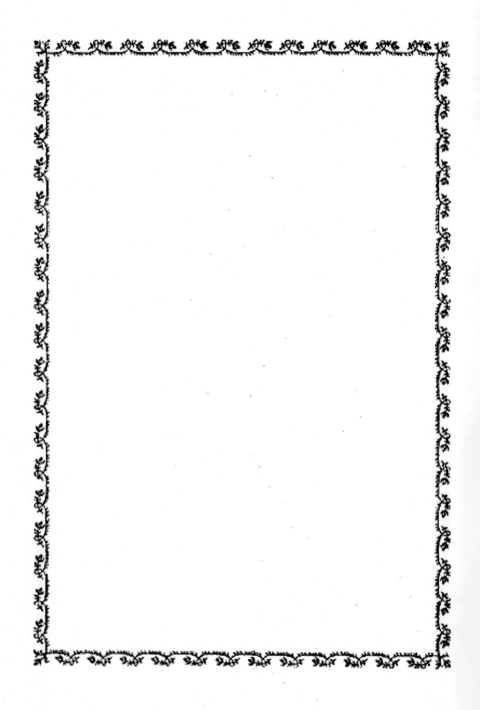

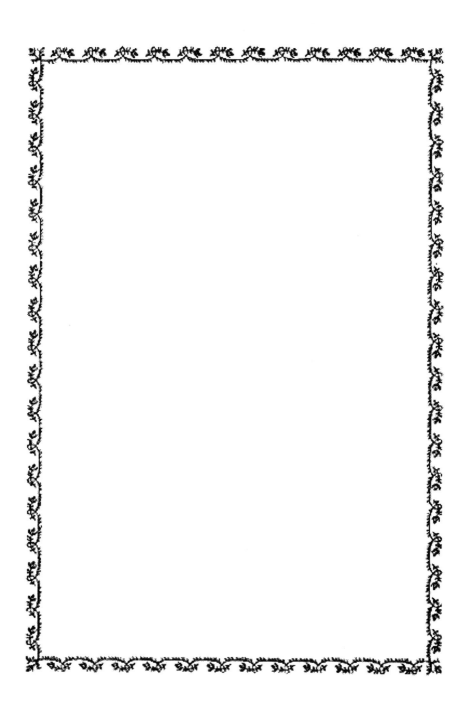

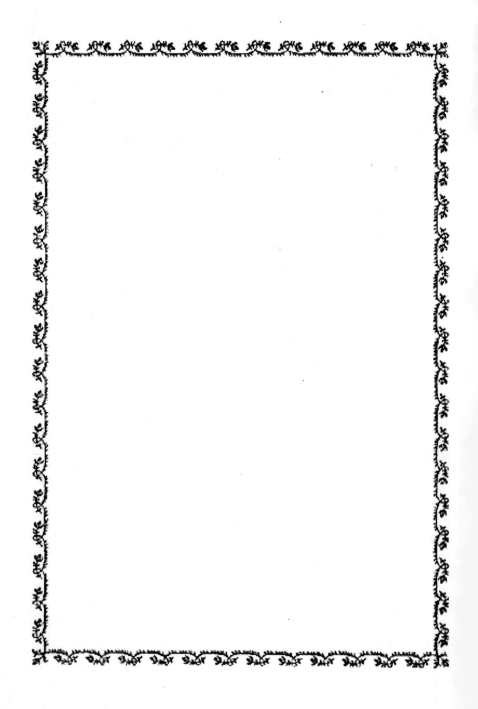

About the Author

Renee Capps has spent many sleepless nights writing about children while on 'babywatch'. Her stories and poems have been sold in children's stores throughout the northwest.

She and her family live on a small farm near Gig Harbor, Washington with "Duke" the horse, and a cat named "Twig".